Gathering Ground:
Art in the E

Marleen Boschen,

Gathering Ground … ects on what cultivating relation … on principles of equity. Ecology, … en living beings and their env… is a term that encompasses the delicate web of connections which sustain us all. The exhibition brings together artistic practices that defend and embrace interconnectedness in our current ecological crisis.

Situated in Tate Modern, *Gathering Ground* invites us to consider the colonial and capitalist afterlives of this building – a gallery housed in a decommissioned oil and coal power station on the banks of the river Thames. The exhibition asks how we can live with and make sense of destruction and loss in the current climate, and how we might develop connections grounded in reciprocity.

The practices of the artists featured in this exhibition are drawn primarily from the Tate Collection. Firmly grounded in land and place, their works deal with issues such as displacement, alongside the destruction of waterways and land due to economic and military interests. Some honour Indigenous knowledges; others highlight strategies for resistance in a precarious world.

Rajesh Vangad and Gauri Gill's collaborative work *The Eye in the Sky* 2016 is based on a photograph by Gill which shows Warli artist Vangad looking out over a sacred mountain in the Dahanu area of Maharashtra, western India. Vangad has added detailed drawings to the photograph, including pictograms of birds and other flying creatures, Warli gods and aircraft. The work reflects on how Indigenous ways of life and protecting the land lie at odds with extractive state and corporate powers.

Carolina Caycedo's *YUMA, Or the Land of Friends II* 2020 deals with the impact of the construction of a mega-dam on Colombia's largest river, the Yuma. By combining and repurposing satellite images, aerial photographs and maps, the work resists exploitative ways of seeing and categorising land and waterways. Caycedo highlights the relational ties that local communities have with the river, understanding it as a political subject with its own agency.

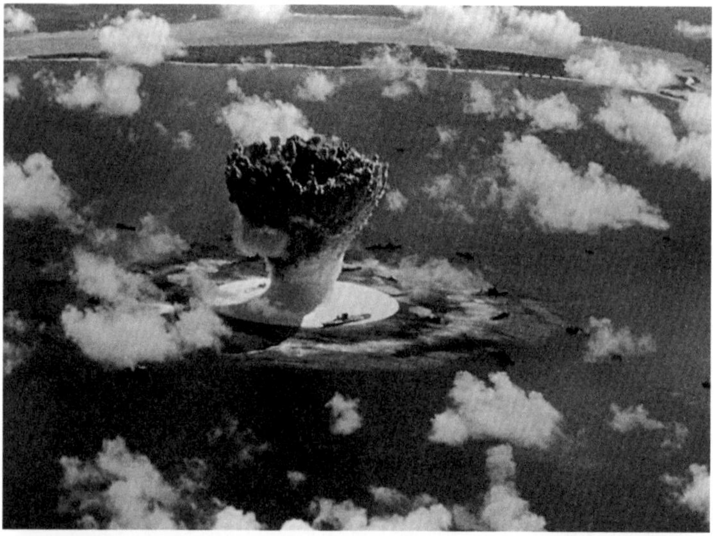

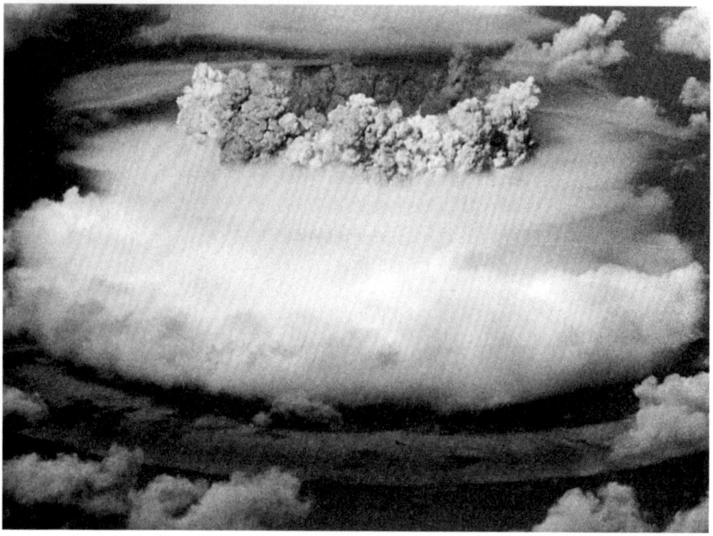

Bruce Conner
CROSSROADS 1976
Film, 35mm, black/white, sound, 37min
Original music by Patrick Gleeson and Terry Riley
Restored by UCLA Film & Television Archive
Courtesy of the Conner Family Trust and Michael Kohn Gallery, Los Angeles

Similarly, in *Study for a Monument* 2022, Abbas Akhavan reconsiders the human-centred focus of monument-making, choosing to commemorate plants instead of people. The work addresses the decades of war and state intervention that have damaged the ecology of the ancient region of Mesopotamia between the Tigris and Euphrates rivers, in present-day Iraq.

Bruce Conner's film *CROSSROADS* 1976 shows replays of the underwater nuclear bomb tests carried out on Bikini Atoll in Aolepān Aorōkin Majel (the Marshall Islands) in 1946. The cumulative force of the testing, which continued until 1958, was 7,000 times that of the atomic bomb dropped on Hiroshima, Japan. Viewed today, the work reveals the devastating impact of nuclear imperialism and compels us to ask whose lifeworlds are deemed disposable.

The issue of violence enacted against land and people is taken up in earnest by Radha D'Souza in her commissioned text for this publication. Challenging the notion of a 'universal human' responsible for climate breakdown, D'Souza situates the separation of nature and culture within a Euro-American worldview and argues that through warfare, militarism and the displacement of Indigenous peoples from their land, we do harm not just to the traditional custodians and protectors of their lands, but to the land itself.

In *Ru K' Ox K'ob'el Jun Ojer Etemab'el* (*The Echo of an Ancient Form of Knowledge*) 2021, Edgar Calel expresses gratitude to his ancestors for their wisdom and guidance. Taking the form of a ritual with stones and fruit, his work challenges individualism and ownership, honouring Maya Kaqchikel philosophy and fostering kinship across time.

Outi Pieski's two hanging works *Guržot ja guovssat* (*Spell on You!*) 2020 and *Skábmavuođđu* (*Spell on Me!*) 2024 resist the erasure of Sámi cultural practices and rights. Pieski's works uphold environmental and matrilineal knowledges threatened by the Nordic colonisation of Sápmi, the traditional territory of the Sámi people. Through the collective practice of *duodji*, she demonstrates how Sámi land is cultural and has co-evolved with humans and other lifeforms across time.

Zheng Bo's *Pteridophilia I* 2016 delves into more-than-human kinship, exploring how to cultivate richer interspecies relationships. Set in a Taiwanese forest, the film shows a series of intimate encounters between queer people and ferns. Provoking important questions about the othering of both plants and people, it challenges us to move beyond binary understandings of gender and the division of human and non-human life.

Through their practice, these artists reflect on ecological breakdown as a crisis of connection. A commissioned text by embodiment facilitator and movement artist Camille Barton takes up questions of interconnection, considering how we can tune in to ourselves, the land and each other. Their text 'Orientating in the Long Dark' invites us to relearn cultures of consent, joy and reciprocity.

At the heart of the exhibition is Abbas Zahedi's sonic installation *Begin Again* 2025, which carves out space for the collective processing of ecological grief. Through his work, including monthly 'support groups', Zahedi reinforces the idea that listening is not a solitary act but a collective, relational practice. In this publication, Zahedi and researcher and sound artist AM Kanngieser discuss how grief sits outside of capitalist time, driven by productivity, and how we might imagine futures built on attunement rather than extraction.

Gathering Ground offers a shared space to imagine more equitable, sustainable and liveable futures. The exhibition approaches gathering as a methodology, grounded in the artists' practices which come together across time and place, where responsibility for the past and the future are interwoven.

Gauri Gill, Rajesh Vangad
The Eye in the Sky 2016 (detail)
From the series *Fields of Sight* 2013–ongoing
Ink on black and white inkjet print photograph on paper
107.6 x 157.3. Tate. Purchased with funds provided by the South Asia Acquisitions Committee 2018. © Gauri Gill, Rajesh Vangad, photo © Raj Salhotra.

What does it mean to be a good custodian?

The artists included in the *Gathering Ground* exhibition were invited to reflect on what being a good custodian or ancestor means to them through the lens of their practices. In what follows, Edgar Calel, Gauri Gill, Zheng Bo, Outi Pieski and Carolina Caycedo share their thoughts on moving through loss and destruction, considering how to build movements rooted in empathy and reciprocity.

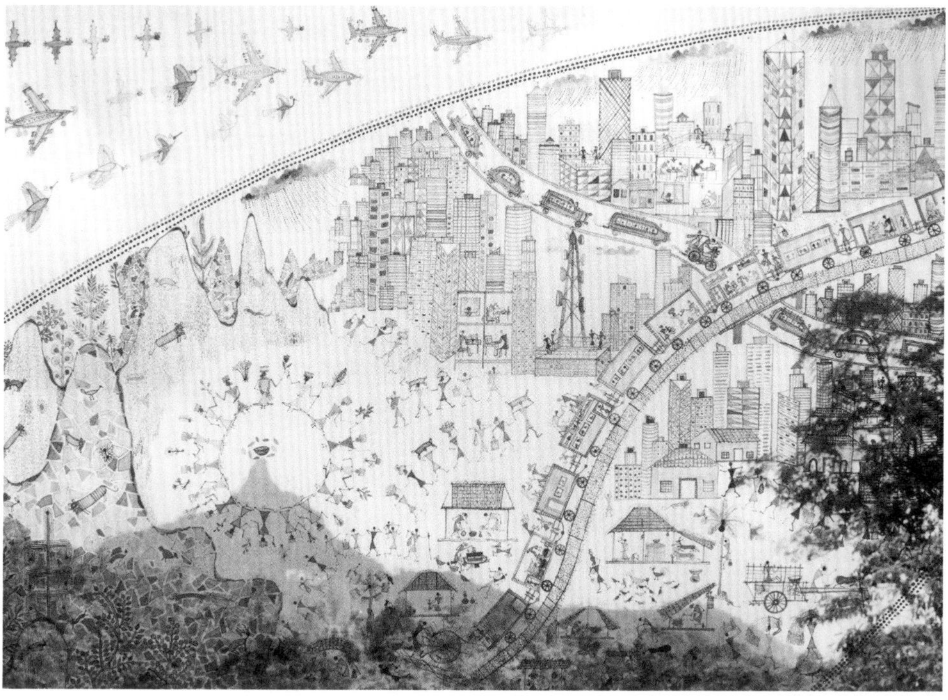

Edgar Calel

In the Kaqchikel community we think that life has only been given to us for a certain period of time and that during that time, as human beings, we carry out an infinite number of actions that leave a mark or footprint on the face of the Earth. Our grandfathers and grandmothers say that we must be in harmony with life and the space where we dwell and transit. In the Kaqchikel community's way of thinking, it is said that everything has life, that everything has a spirit and an owner. Time and space are the basis of this knowledge. From this wisdom that has been transmitted from generation to generation comes the awareness of making offerings to the Ancestors, to the guardians of life, and to the places where the grandmothers and grandfathers left their knowledge and practices sown in us in order to give continuity to life. With respect and through these practices we will be able to maintain our connection with the Earth and the universe.

We need to be aware that we are just another part of everything that exists on Earth, and that we are interconnected with each other. We must think that we are also the rivers, the stones, the trees and the mountains. We must take our flight like birds. We must work more as a collective just like the ants, and protect our territory with the claws of the jaguar.

Nature has always been generous with everyone. I think we should learn from it. We should be more generous and humble like a tree, which bears fruit and offers its shade to those who need and want it. It is complex to think about healing and treating the wounds of the territory while the face of the Earth continues to be perforated, day and night, in order to extract its properties. Every day, extractivist corporations attack and drive away the spirits that guard and inhabit the surfaces and depths of our Mother Earth. We need to stop and think in other ways – ways in which respect for life and nature are the basis of our existence – to give continuity to our lives and activities. I believe that as long as people continue to think in an individualistic way it will be extremely difficult to overcome all the physical, spiritual and intellectual illnesses that are dispersed in the air when we aspire to a modern way of life and progress.

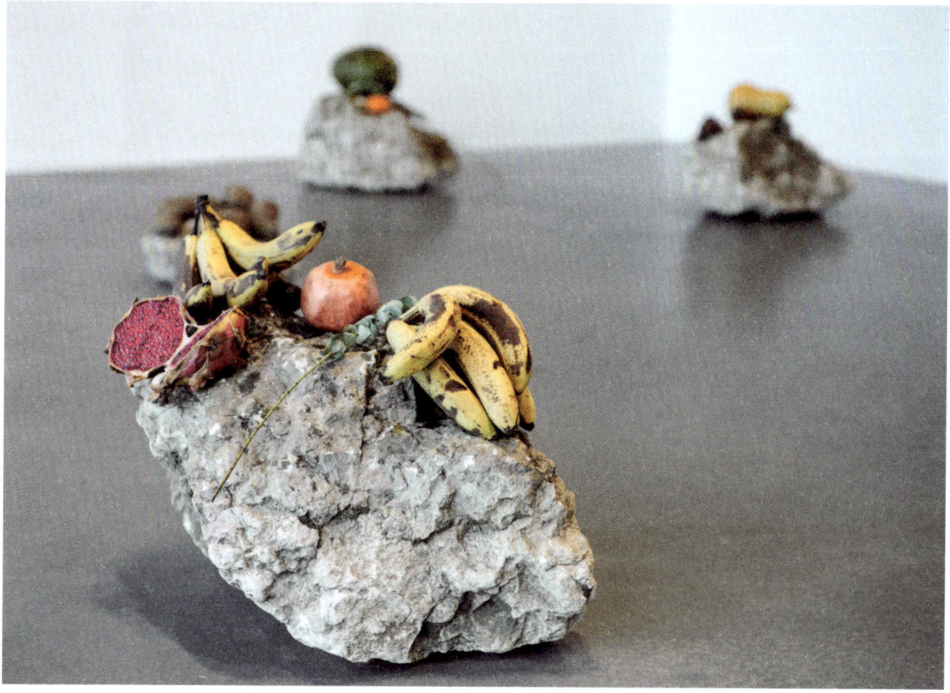

Edgar Calel
Ru K' Ox K'ob'el Jun Ojer Etemab'el (*The Echo of an Ancient Form of Knowledge*) 2021
Performance, 1 person, rocks, fruit and vegetables
Lent by Edgar Çalel with support from the 2021 Frieze Tate Fund supported by Endeavor to benefit the Tate collection 2023. © Edgar Calel, photo © Tate Photography (Reece Straw). See also pp,8–9.

Edgar Calel is an artist working in a variety of media, exploring the complexities of the Indigenous experience, as seen through the Mayan Kaqchikel practices and beliefs, in juxtaposition with the systematic racism and exclusion that the Indigenous people of Guatemala endure.

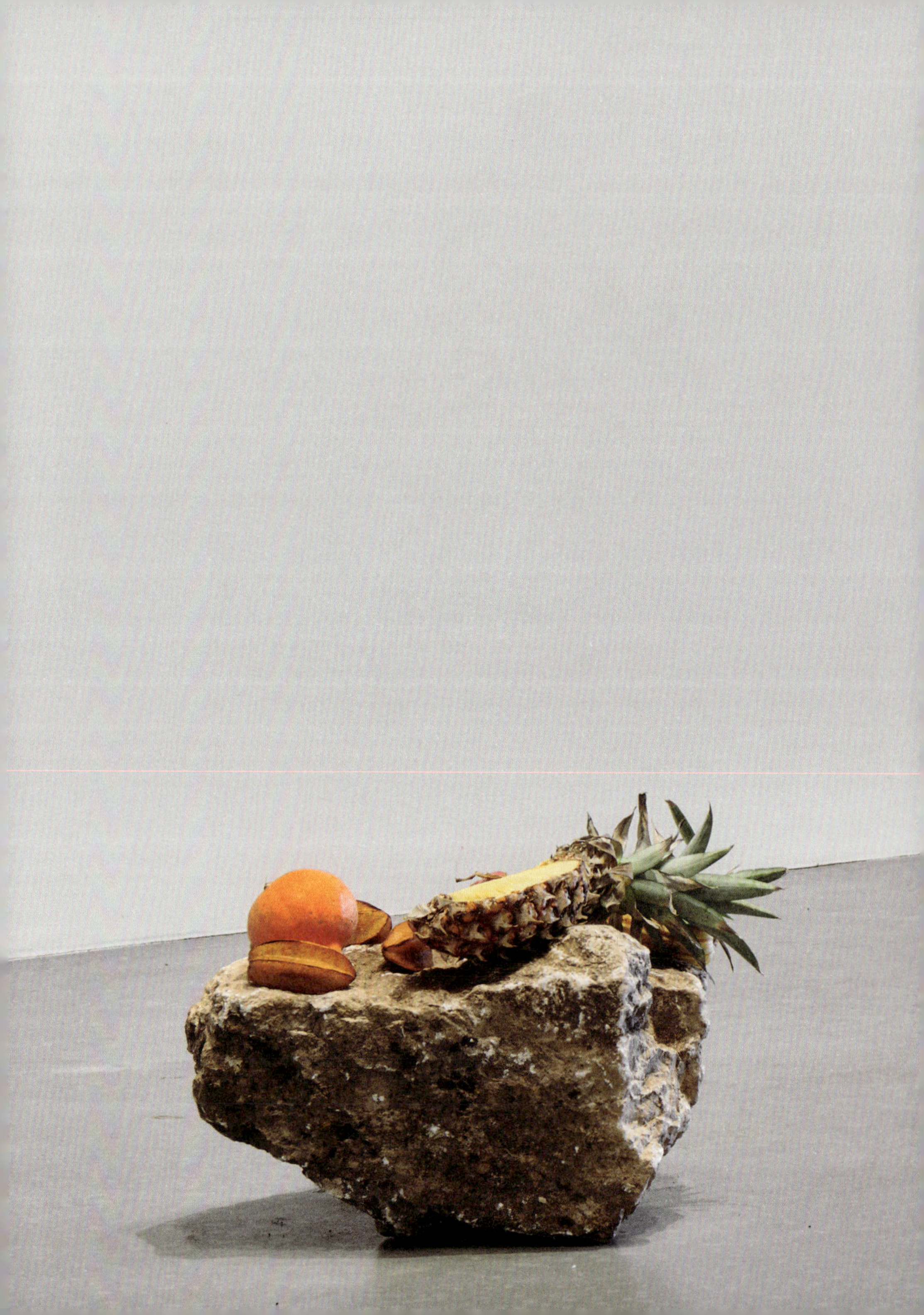

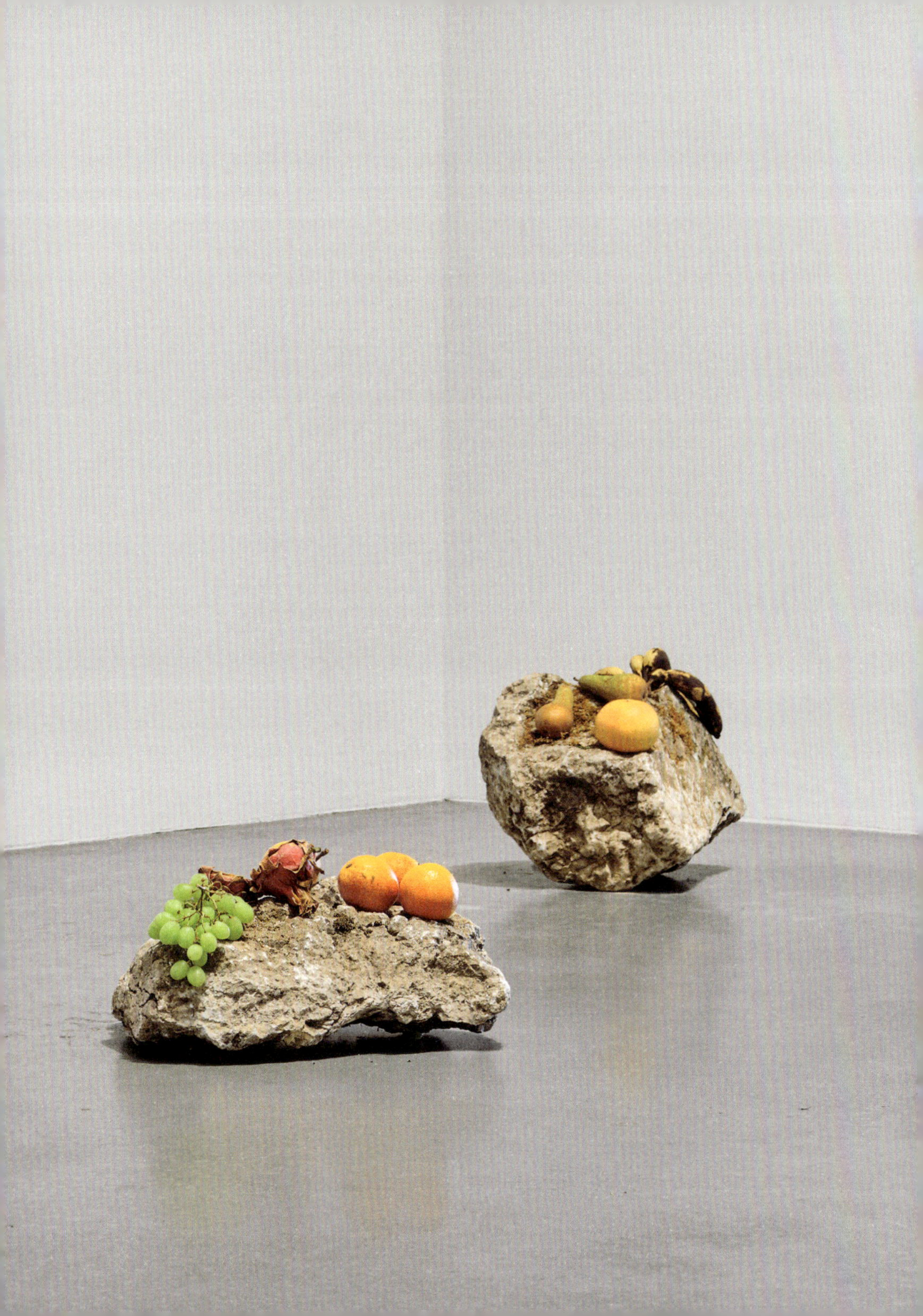

Gauri Gill

We live in a desperately unequal world, and one that is exclusionary. I am a photographer living in New Delhi, and have spent close to three decades working with and visiting friends who are rural, Indigenous, women, migrant or immigrant, from denotified tribes, or religious minorities. For me, photography can be a kind of listening device to acknowledge those without voice, or visibility. While photography is a democratic medium in some respects, as almost everyone today has access to some form of camera, there is disproportionate power in terms of who gets to tell the story. My own small attempt has been to try and cede control of representation and of individualisation; to get myself out of the way in order to see more clearly, and collectively. Because photography can help us not only to broaden monolithic representations, but also to expand closed and self-referential circles, with their limited and insular understandings.

Paying attention might reveal the so-called extraordinary to be banal, the mundane to be spectacular, and the singular to be plural. When I focus only on the explicit object – which itself is constantly changing – I fail to pay heed to all of the infinite processes and players embedded in it. Even in attempting to deconstruct the process I end up creating new centres of focus. In truth, there is a multitude behind any apparently singular act – or any solidified convergence of acts that may appear in the form of an object, place or person. And there is an ever-flowing inter-dependent continuum, each instant following naturally from what came before.

Empathy therefore can only ever be akin to the empathy of the right hand for the left hand – seeing no inherent difference except for the possible and changing circumstances faced by each. Where and towards whom we direct our attention is an act of love, and belief. At the heart of my endeavour has been a great admiration for the unique survival strategies employed by people in precarity, and a desire to witness and share those ways. Be it play, humour, creativity, or acts of tender beauty, I wish to honour the ingenious ways people in deep waters find to swim, or stay afloat.

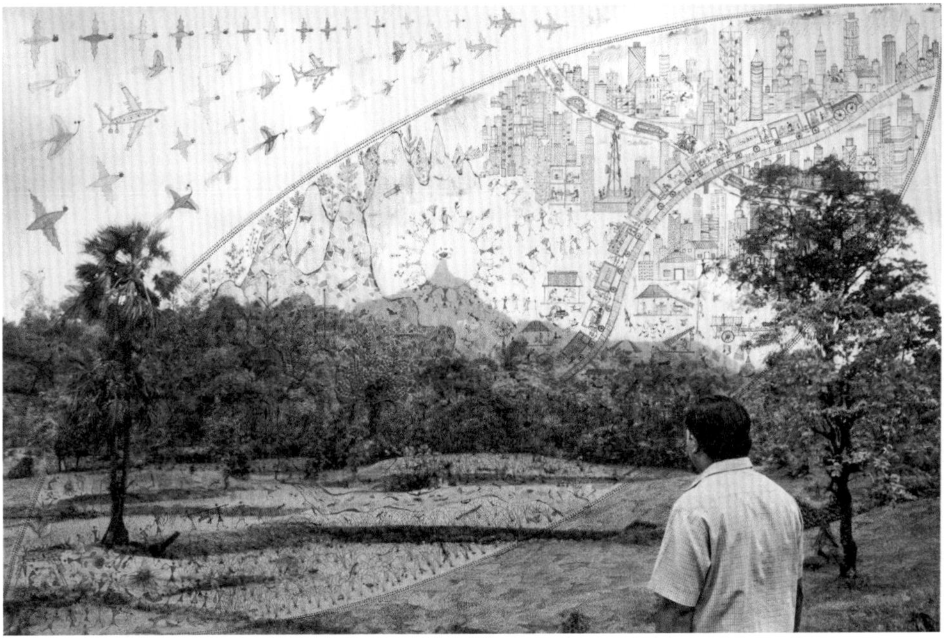

Gauri Gill, Rajesh Vangad
The Eye in the Sky 2016
From the series *Fields of Sight* 2013–ongoing
Ink on black and white inkjet print photograph on paper
107.6 x 157.3. Tate. Purchased with funds provided by the South Asia Acquisitions Committee 2018.
© Gauri Gill, Rajesh Vangad, photo © Raj Salhotra.

Gauri Gill is a Delhi-based photographer. Gill's work addresses the Indian identity markers of caste, class and community.

Rajesh Vangad is a Warli painter, a traditional form of painting belonging to the Indigenous people of Warli, India.

Zheng Bo

In 2016, a botanist took me to a forest on the outskirts of Taipei, where he and other scientists study ferns. Since then I have been going there to make this unending film, *Pteridophilia*.

I always look forward to going back to the forest because the air is so invigorating. We usually go up the hill in the early morning, half awake. Once in the forest, bathing in the sea of oxygen and phytoncides, our bodies and minds reach a heightened level of agility and attentiveness. Plants reveal to us the full potential of a three-dimensional space. Massive bird's-nest ferns perch on trees. Tiny mosses blanket rocks. The light is dramatic, the sound rich and the aroma intense. The assemblage has a distinct style, yet is constantly changing. This forest is better than any artwork I could ever make.

I have lived on Earth for fifty years, and I'm still learning how to live a good life on our planet, a life that is ecologically just, vibrant and beautiful. Over the past twelve years, plants have been my main teachers: ferns in Taiwan, mosses in Scandinavia, grass trees in Western Australia, date palms in the Arabian Peninsula. I've learned to think in epochs, not minutes. I've learned to sense fragrance, complexity, and gravity. I've learned to appreciate forces larger than us, beyond us. I want to bond with beautiful beings around me, not just intellectually, but somatically. Becoming intimate with 萬物 *wanwu* – myriad happenings – has perhaps made my life less clean, less predictable, but definitely more alive.

Zheng Bo is an artist based in Hong Kong and New Caledonia-Kanaky.

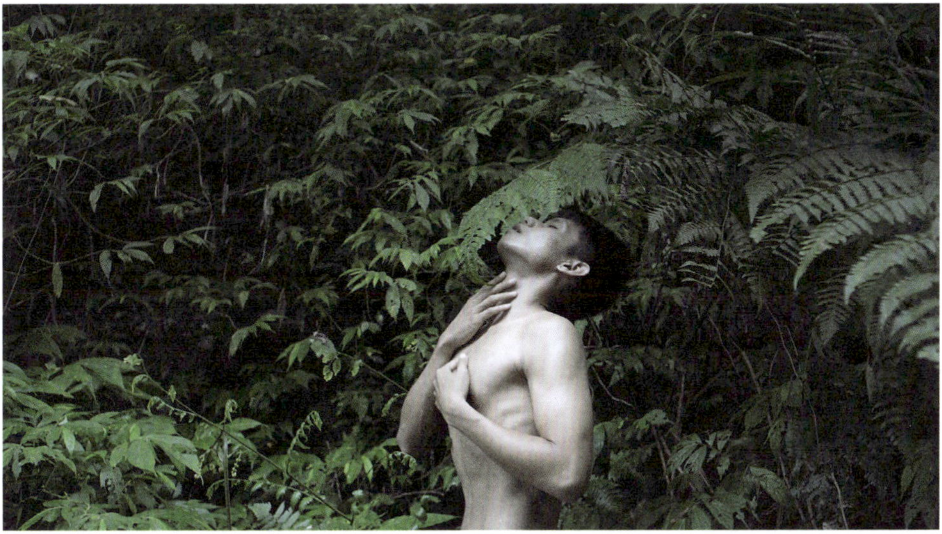

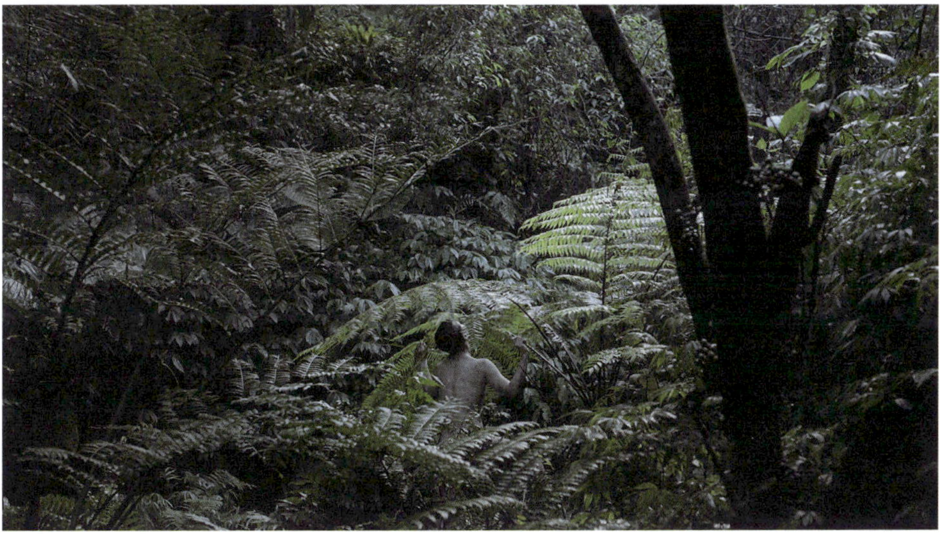

Zheng Bo
Pteridophilia / 2016
Video, colour and sound (mono)
17min. Tate. Purchased with funds provided by the Asia-Pacific Acquisitions Committee 2024

Outi Pieski

Combining traditional *duodji* (Sámi arts and crafts), and often created collectively, my work aims to revitalise women's traditions and to open intergenerational dialogues about revitalisation, rematriation and the biocultural reality of the Sámi people. My work references social gathering, kinship and collective creativity. Laboriously handwoven knots represent a matriarchal counterforce to a competitive, individual-centred society. They raise questions about ancestral return, Indigenous peoples' rights and the relationship between humans, animals and land. The installations create a spiritual forest that carries wisdom and a variety of contradictory forces: fears, wishes and desires.

Duodji is a holistic concept that preserves the Sámi philosophy, values and spirituality, and connects them with practical and traditional skills. There is a somatic aspect to *duodji*: the practice brings out things that we hold in our bodies, including intergenerational traumas – but with this also comes the wisdom of our Ancestors. Often when you are learning *duodji* your hands remember, even though you weren't aware you knew how. There is a ritual aspect to tassel-making; the process is very repetitive and natural, the feeling similar to the one you have when walking or skiing. It's like a practical way of synchronising with the rhythm of other living entities.

Indigenous people are forced to play a significant role in responding to the climate crisis, since the last remaining biodiversity hotspots are in our areas. There is currently huge international interest in the exploitation of the natural resources of the Arctic regions. In Sápmi, the land of the Sámi, we are living in a new wave of eco-colonialism, in which the aim is to take over these lands by establishing new mines and wind power industry, in the name of sustainable development. Many industrial developments have already been built in Sámi homelands, terminating land rights, routes and habitats. The problems of so-called minority cultures are intertwined and, on a global level, ultimately linked to nature conservation issues. When we open our ears to the marginalised 'minority' representatives in our society, we increase our awareness of issues that are relevant to everyone.

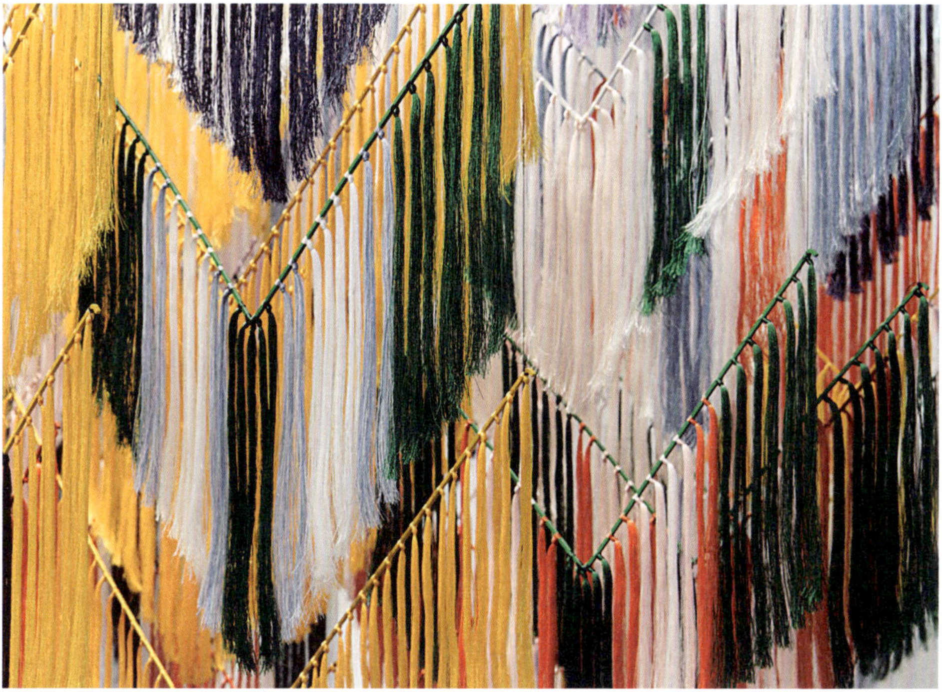

Outi Pieski
Guržot ja guovssat (*Spell on You!*) 2020, (detail)
overleaf: *Skábmavuođđu* (*Spell on Me!*) 2024
Synthetic thread, steel, wood and paint, dimensions variable.
Tate. Purchased with funds provided by the AKO Foundation Acquisition Fund for Indigenous Art from Northern Europe 2024,
© Outi Pieski, photo © Tate Photography (Reece Straw)

Outi Pieski is a Sámi artist based in Ohcejohka (Utsjoki), Finland. Through painting, printmaking, photography, video and installation, Pieski explores the relationship between humans and their environment, raising questions around ancestral knowledge and Indigenous peoples' rights.

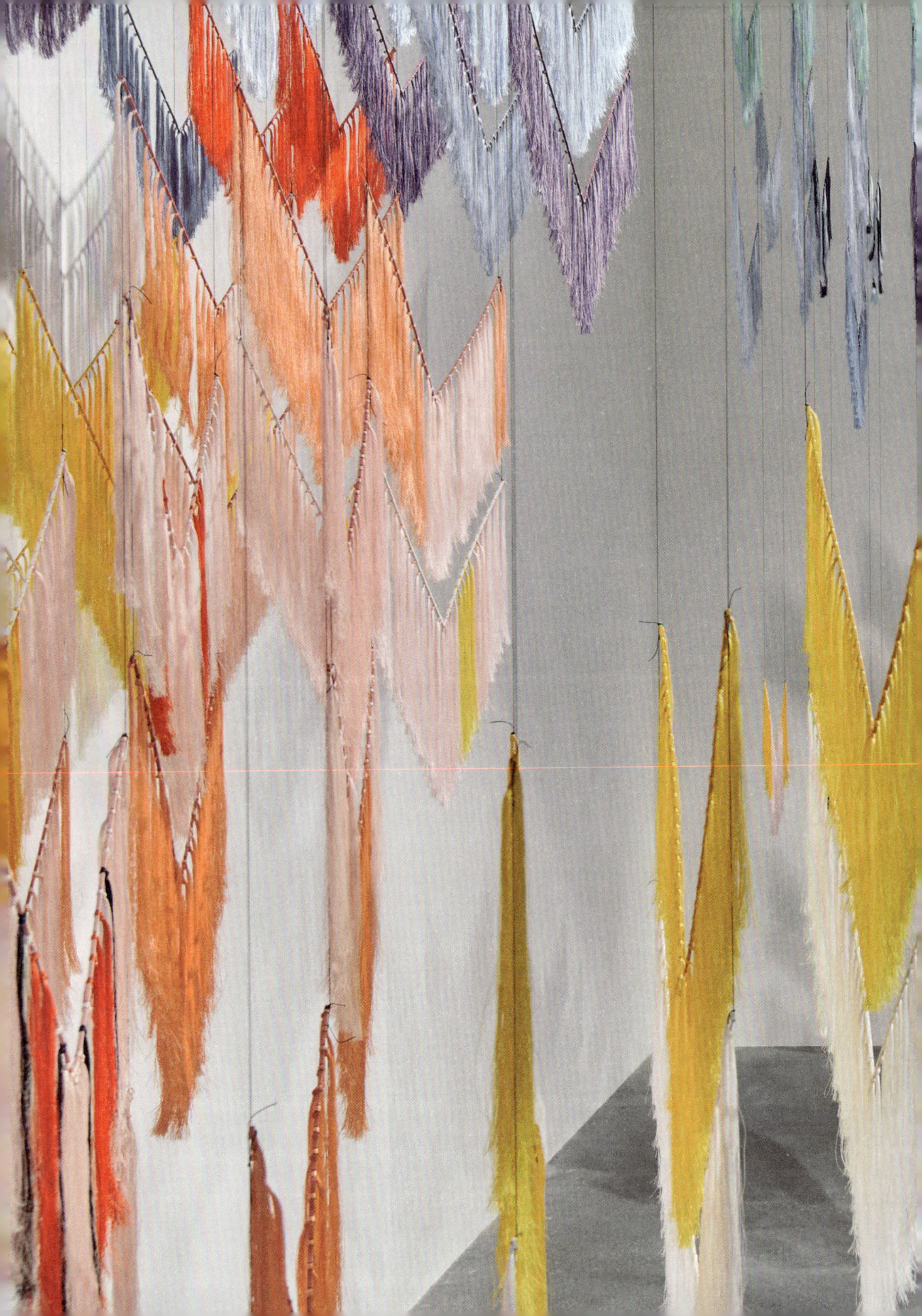

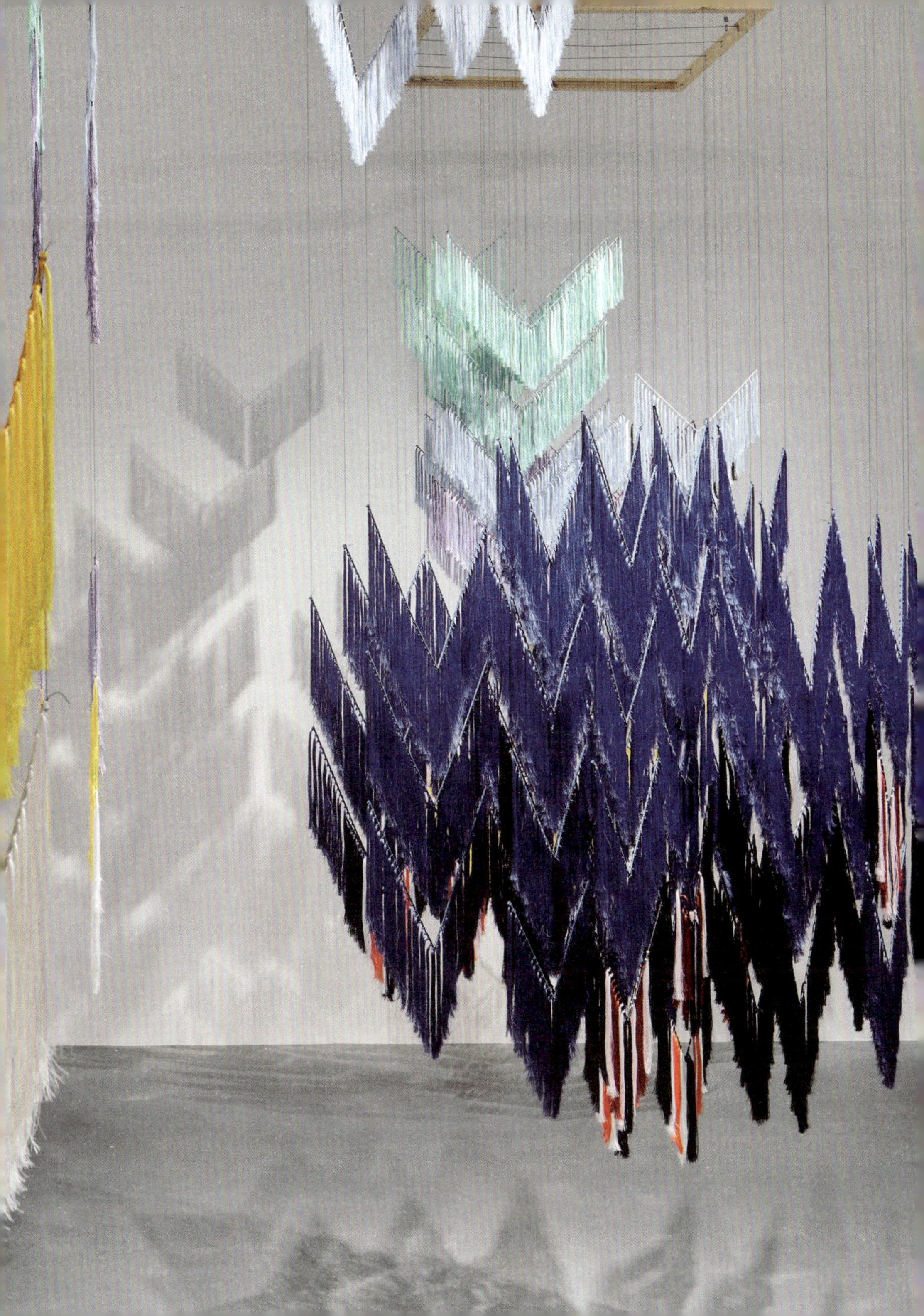

Carolina Caycedo

How do we hack the view from above?
the colonial gaze of those who look down on us?
the optical sight of the drone that bombs us?
the satellite perspective that looks to erase us, that blurs our humanity?
the google map that truncates our visual memory?
the landscapes that render our lands as empty?

We dig hands into the soil
deeper and deeper into the ground
the dirt under our fingernails
and in the creases of our knees
becomes our magic

We throw shoes and clothes away
waddle into our rivers
the current strong between our thighs
licks our insides
moisturising our feeling-thinking

We cradle our seeds in handwoven bags
trade them with sisters across the hemisphere
to draw up the elements that govern the four directions

Into the wetlands we weave our legs and arms
we walk with moss, marshes and mangroves
with our toes and fingers we play with baby goby fish
our fingers caress roots of sphagnum
our feet get swallowed by the mushy bottom
and spat out again while we moan in pleasure

We chew sweet and juicy mangos
let'em drip down our neck and nipples
with the same ease that we undam rivers
and liberate our lands and waters

We embody our most profound desires, our most urgent demands
Our quena and zampoña flutes
well guarded in our mochilas
see the light of moon and fire
We blow life into them, chewing our coca leaves
licking our tobacco honey
eating our peyote, playing our drums
We pray, sing and dance at the rhythm of our earth's heartbeat
our steps calling our ancestors past and future
"We are alive! We are alive! We remember, come dance with us!"

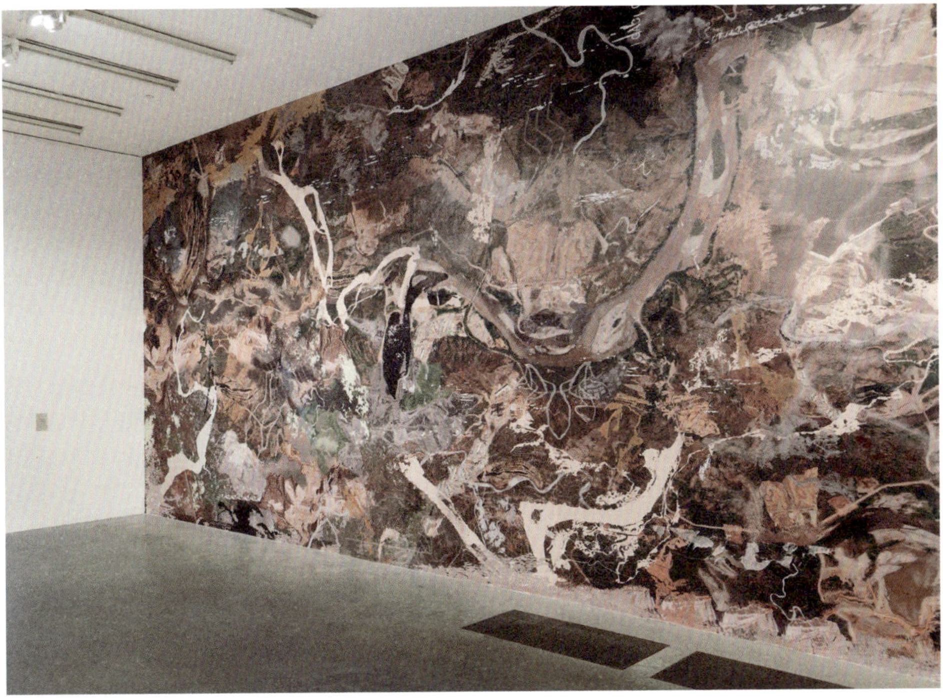

Carolina Caycedo
YUMA, Or the Land of Friends II 2020
Satellite photo collage mural
© Carolina Caycedo, courtesy of the artist
photo © Tate Photography (Reece Straw). See also p. 31.

Carolina Caycedo is a multimedia artist. Process and participation are central to Caycedo's practice, and she contributes to the reconstruction of environmental and historical memory as a fundamental space for climate and social justice.

In Dialogue: Abbas Zahedi and AM Kanngieser

AM Kanngieser

While we approach questions of crisis and grief somewhat differently, what draws me to your work is a shared concern with what an ethic of listening could mean. Can you talk about what first drew you to make *Begin Again*, and what it means for you?

Abbas Zahedi

The origins of *Begin Again* relate to an ongoing entanglement with personal loss and the broader structural violences that shape experiences of grief and dispossession – from the geopolitical conditions that resulted in the loss of my parents at a young age, to the death of my disabled younger brother, whom I cared for long-term, to the enduring trauma of the Grenfell Tower fire. These events not only shaped my relationship with mourning but also made visible the systemic nature of loss itself. In these instances, grief was not reducible to a singular event but extended across social and infrastructural layers, determining which lives are rendered vulnerable and how grieving is collectively mediated.

In *Begin Again*, I consciously avoid portraying this grief as a state of affect and instead interpret it as an ecological and infrastructural condition. This approach rejects the reduction of mourning to emotional registers and instead situates it within a broad framework of relationality. *Begin Again* treats grief not as a subjective experience, but as an ambient force that is spatial, vibrational and historically layered over time.

The concept behind the installation was to embed resonant sculptures into the utility pipes of Tate Modern, bringing the 'guts' of this former power station into the gallery space. Pipes that typically serve as conduits for extracting and redirecting resources are transformed into a series of resonant thresholds. These vibrations are not just sonic, but indicate a more extensive system – echoes of histories that persist in the present. If sound can be said to map power relations, then *Begin Again* becomes a platform for listening differently, making audible the structural conditions that shape grief across bodies, spaces and temporalities.

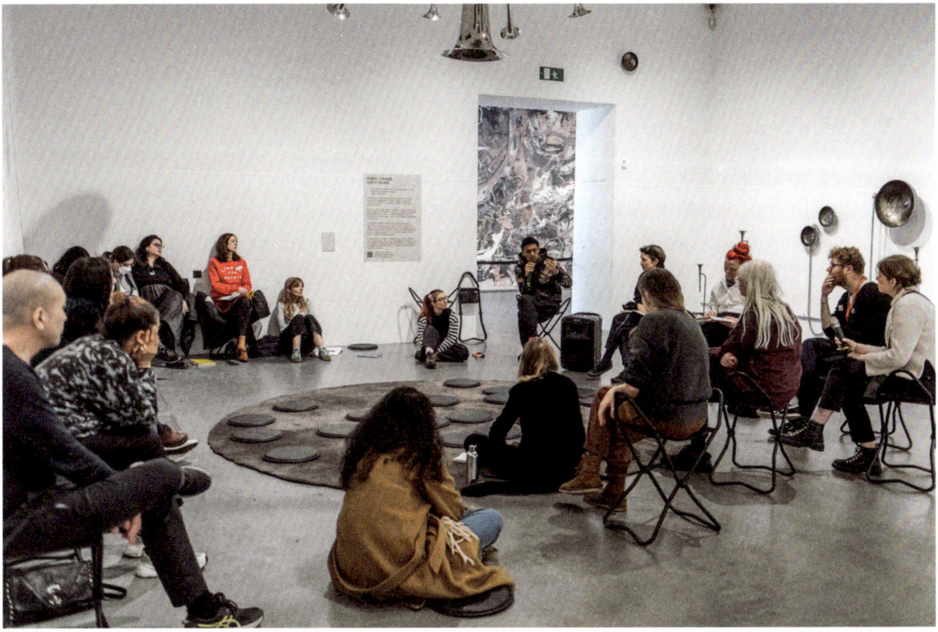

Abbas Zahedi hosting a support group for the collective processing of ecological grief in Tate Modern, 2025.
Photo © Tate Photography (Luana Burton)

In your work, sound is not a neutral aesthetic experience, and listening is not a passive act but an ethical and political practice that necessitates awareness of power relations, colonial histories and ecological violence. In my work, too, infrastructural sound is not just about the materiality of pipes and buildings but about how listening is always a political act, and how institutions condition what can be heard and what remains inaudible.

AMK I have been collaborating for many years with frontline Indigenous Pacific communities, particularly women, queer and transgender people, on projects centring self-determination and sovereignty in a time of ecocide. The immersive work *Oceanic Refractions*, on which I collaborated with Mere Nailatikau, situates the contemporary condition within long spiritual and ancestral lineages of knowing and being in relation. How does *Begin Again* engage with contemporary artistic movements – particularly those led by Black and Indigenous women, disabled artists, and nonbinary and transgender creators – that explore themes of grief, ecological connection, rest and community building?

AZ Grief operates outside of capitalist time. The experience of mourning disrupts rhythms of productivity. Practices of collective mourning and radical care necessitate exiting the neoliberal impetus to function at all costs. The movements you refer to have been central in reorientating grief not as an isolated event but as a structural and historical condition, and showing that the marginalisation of vulnerable communities is a requirement for dominant structures to persist uninhibited. Christina Sharpe's 'wake work' is particularly pertinent to this sense of personal and collective loss: the wake is both an oceanic space and an ongoing temporal condition that extends the afterlives of slavery into the present. In *Begin Again*, this sense of seismic resonance operates as a spatial and temporal force, registering how grief moves across scales, from the personal to the planetary.

This work also speaks to the disability justice movement's emphasis on alternative temporalities. For example, Leah Lakshmi Piepzna-Samarasinha critiques how ableist structures demand productivity even in grief, refusing the need for rest, reflection and collective mourning. *Gathering Ground* counters this imperative, resisting the conventional timescales of exhibitions, for example by encouraging visitors to slow down in *Begin Again.*

AMK I'm interested in your term 'seismic resonance' and how this relates to the idea of sound as embedded within power, making audible the relationship between people and infrastructures. We can see how sound can be used to both trace out and be traced through the material geographies of power, as in Israel's use of sonic warfare against Palestinians, and the violence of dispossession in the Pacific. What does this audibility mean when listening to a building? How do listeners hear themselves in relation?

AZ Seismic resonance functions as a form of affective transmission, through which the deeper structures shaping our environments – both material and ideological – become available to sensation. Following your argument that sound maps colonial and environmental violence, *Begin Again* suggests that listening must go beyond perception to become an ethical and political engagement with space, an encounter with the vibrational memory of that space, an attunement to the latent intensities within. Rather than occupying the conventional position of an observer, I want the gallery visitor to be pulled in by the generative and unpredictable soundscape of the work and to become part of the same vibratory system as the structure itself. The sound

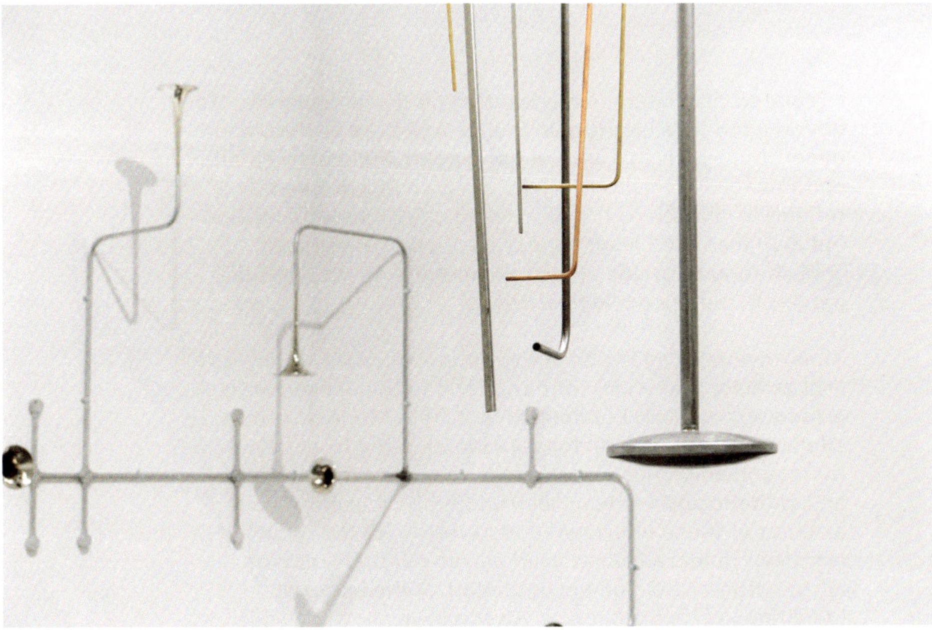

Installation photography of Abbas Zahedi, *Begin Again* 2025 as part of *Gathering Ground* at Tate Modern, 2025. Photo © Tate Photography (Luana Burton)

waves travelling through the museum's pipes repurpose its architecture as a structure that does not merely preserve but amplifies, disrupts and resists erasure. Similarly, the carpeted area within the installation marks a space for gathering, reinforcing the idea that listening is not a solitary act but a collective, relational practice. Audio inputs in the gallery wall allow anyone with amplified instruments or vocals to engage with the installation – to tune in, disrupt, collapse or riff off its sonic artifice – further destabilising the hierarchy between artwork and audience, composer and interpreter, structure and resonance. Instead of a closed composition, therefore, the installation becomes an open system where things can continually unfold, shift and be reconfigured through participation.

AMK In this context, how do the sounds we hear in Tate Modern connect us to its complex history, particularly its connections to British colonialism and sugar plantations?

AZ Tate Modern occupies the shell of the Bankside Power Station, a structure originally designed to convert fossil fuels into energy – a process mirroring the broader imperial logic whereby energy, labour and raw materials were extracted from colonised regions, processed into commodities and circulated through the arteries of capital accumulation. More directly, the Tate institution itself is indebted to the wealth generated by Henry Tate's sugar empire, an industry built on the backs of enslaved labourers in the Caribbean. The refinery's operations not only relied on human exploitation but also reshaped landscapes, exhausting soils and contributing to cycles of environmental degradation that persist in today's ecological crises.

These overlapping logics of extraction – contemporary as well as historical – are not peripheral to the conversation on ecology and art, but central to it. Tate Modern's physical site and institutional history are inextricable from colonial extraction and industrial capitalist histories, and as both an aesthetic and financial institution, the museum is an artefact of these intertwined histories – yet the realities are often rendered silent amid narratives that treat art as an autonomous domain untainted by the material conditions of its production. As you have shown in your work, listening can serve as a practice of restitution – not through representation, but as reverberation. If Tate Modern's pipes once transported the residues of the colonial industry, their vibrations in *Begin Again* seek to repurpose this infrastructure, transforming the building into a site of historical witnessing.

In his critique of capitalism, Jason Hickel argues that ecological collapse is not an incidental byproduct of industrialisation but a direct consequence of colonial land dispossession. The crisis we face today emerges from a centuries-long history of treating land, labour and life as extractable commodities. Through the perceptual training that is a part of coloniality, we have been conditioned to relate dispassionately to 'nature' and the Indigenous communities positioned as its stewards through our reliance on urban infrastructures. The idea that certain people live within 'nature' while others live in cities reinforces an extractive paradigm that treats land and resources as passive reserves, external to modernity and available for depletion. I don't see a way of resolving this crisis through making representational work. Instead, I want to situate listeners within the conditions that have produced it and, by listening, to enter into an act of accountability.

AMK Your point about coloniality being a perceptual training – a way of organising our relationships with land, bodies and global systems – resonates with me. In recounting my work in Oceania to people in places like the United Kingdom, I have come to understand that the scale and temporality of ecological grief are undeniably different across different ecosystems. Given that the Earth is not lost for all of us in the same ways, on the same scales, at the same times, how do you anticipate listening and sound will move people in the UK to 'imagine new frameworks' to restore ecological connectivity?

AZ I began working with sound in this way in response to the Grenfell fire, when I was mourning the recent death of a dear friend, peer and neighbour, Khadija Saye. The fire was not just a singular catastrophe but a violent rupture which exposed the underlying structural conditions of racialised neglect, state abandonment and economic disparity that had already shaped the lives of those of us growing up in those conditions. How grief unfolded in the aftermath of the blaze – how it was mediated, who was heard, and whose loss was rendered politically inconvenient – deeply informed my understanding of how infrastructure, history and systems of power condition mourning.

In this space of loss, displacement and dispossession, I began thinking through how sound might serve as a medium for collective grief – not as an attempt to 'heal' or resolve, but as a way of holding space for its resonances, for its refusal to be neatly assimilated into the language of closure or the visual neatness of an art space. Rather than treating the climate crisis as abstract or distant, *Begin Again* foregrounds being-in-crisis as a lived, vibrational condition that permeates bodies, infrastructures and geographies in ways that exceed conventional representation. This is where listening, as a practice, fundamentally differs from the visual dominance of many ecological discourses, which often privilege legibility, measurement and quantification. Listening, by contrast, moves across registers, unsettling and reconfiguring the listener's relation to space and time, and re-centring imagination as a force for change.

(overleaf) Abbas Zahedi hosting a support group for the collective processing of ecological grief in Tate Modern, 2025. Photo © Tate Photography (Luana Burton)

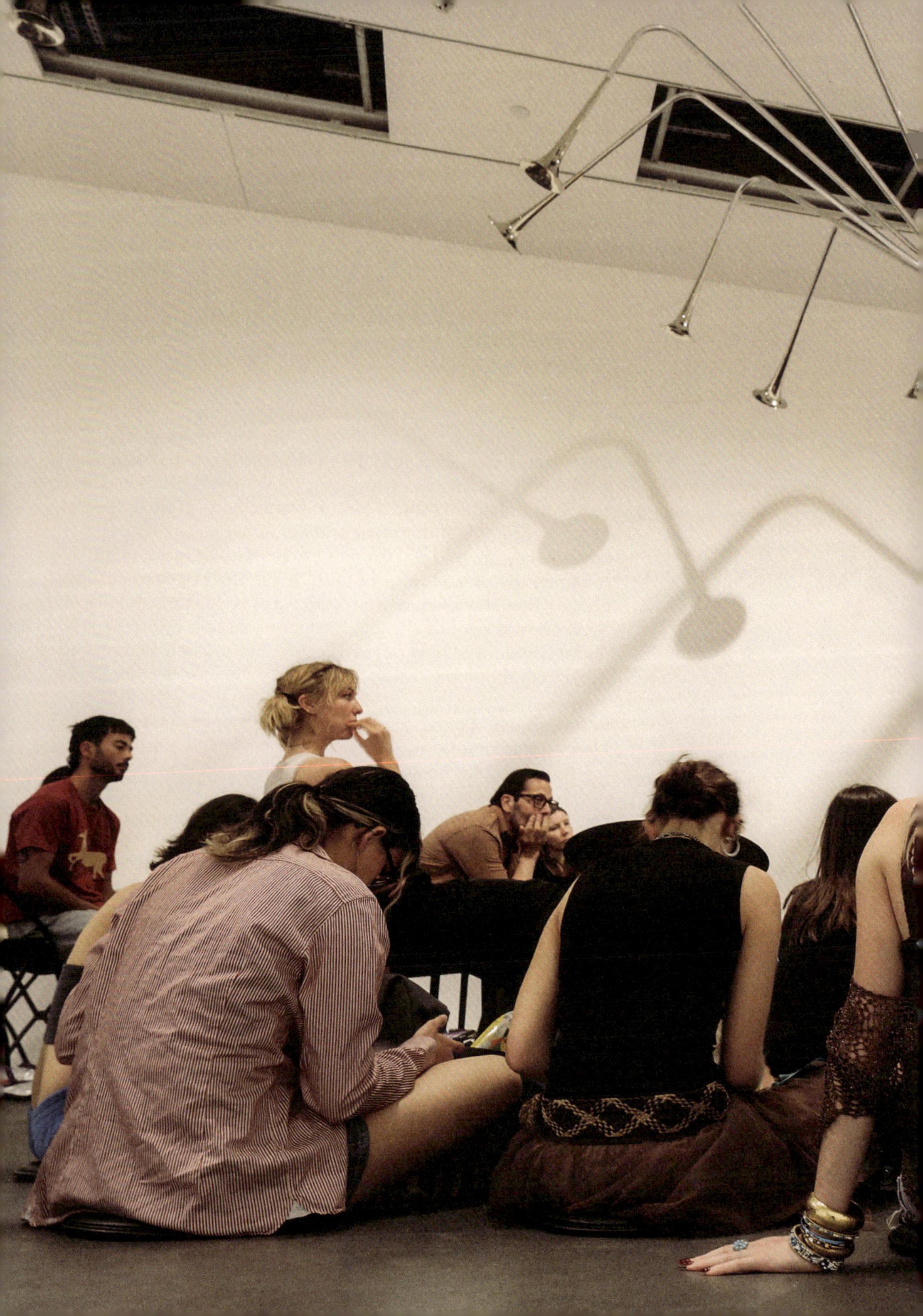

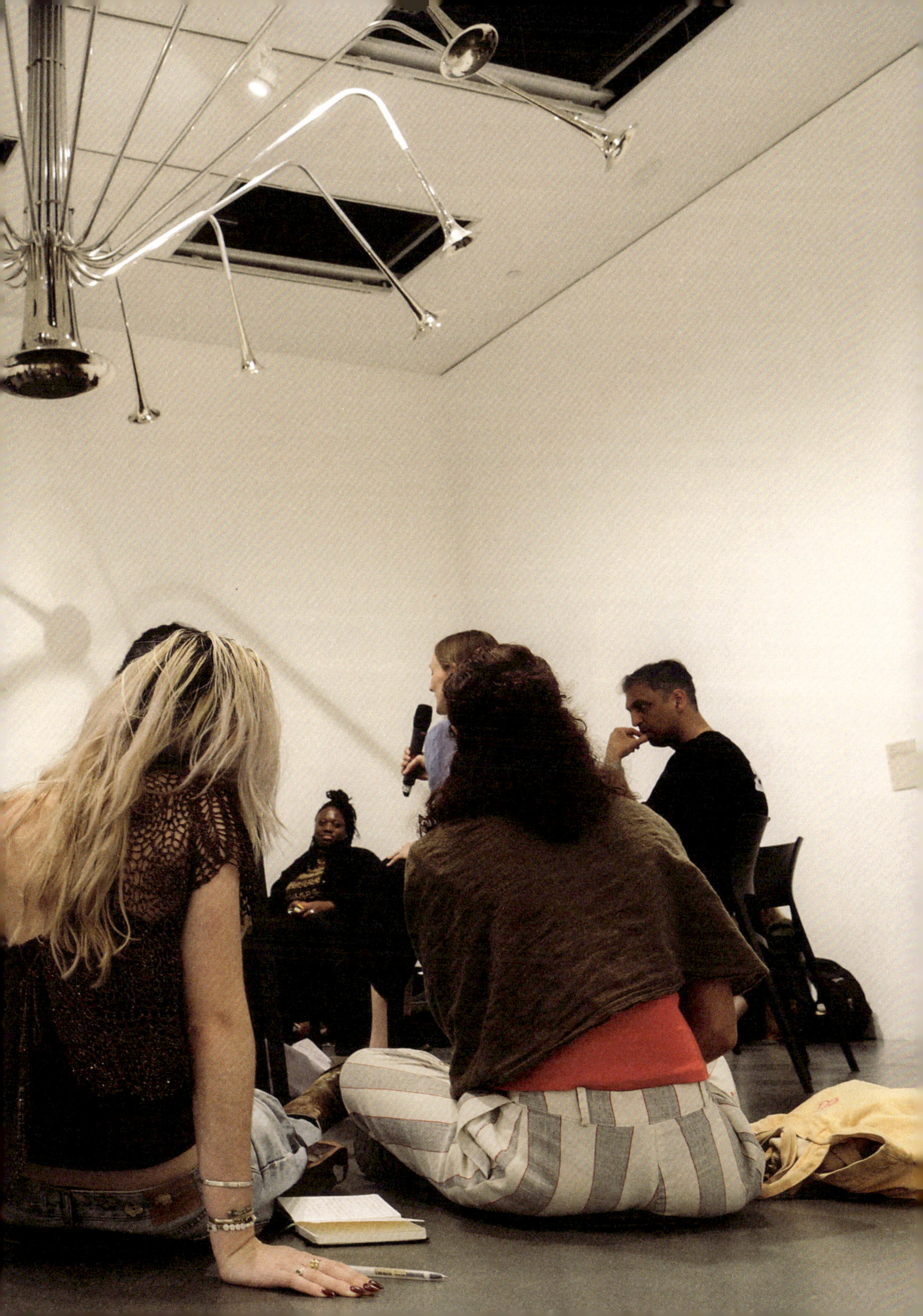

A year-long public programme accompanying *Begin Again* allows for the inclusion of monthly support groups within the space itself. Prioritising presence over resolution, these groups will function as sites of what Stefano Harney and Fred Moten term undercommons – spaces of fugitive planning, where participants can collectively navigate the discontinuities, dissonances and temporal disruptions that characterise ecological grief. Your experience of working with Indigenous Pacific communities highlights the stark disparities in how ecological collapse is experienced, narrated and metabolised: while frontline communities are already in the midst of existential loss – territories sinking, traditional ecological knowledge disrupted, entire ways of life disappearing – those in places like the UK experience climate collapse as abstract, unreal, elsewhere. And your argument that listening, practised ethically, can serve as a way of situating oneself within systems of harm resonates deeply with me.

Listening resists the flattening of ecological grief into a universal condition, demanding that we remain attentive to the specificities of loss. In this way, *Begin Again* offers not closure but a practice of staying with the trouble, in Donna Haraway's formulation: a commitment to remaining with the discomfort, listening expansively, imagining futures predicated not on extraction but on mutual attunement. The challenge is not merely to listen but to listen differently: to listen with the weight of history, to listen with the knowledge that larger forces always structure grief, and to begin again – not as a return to what was, but as an emergence towards what might still be composable.

Abbas Zahedi is an interdisciplinary artist and educator. Zahedi reflects on the interconnectedness of ecological, cultural and human systems.

AM Kanngieser is an award-winning geographer and sound artist, working through listening and attunement to approach the relations between people, place and ecologies.

Orientating in the long dark

Camille Barton

In whose footsteps do we follow? At present, the greed of multinational corporations marches us towards collective harm and doom. Can we slow down enough to pivot and find another path? Can we listen deeply to elders, cultures and beings that embody reciprocity with the web of life? Can we learn to sing a different song? To vibrate with the hum of the collective, treat earth with reverence? Disrupt the high-pitched frequencies and drilling of extraction and domination, in an act of service for our planet that loves us so deeply?

How deep is our love? If the most accessible emotion we feel on beholding our environment is fear – the fear of extinction – perhaps we need to learn to love again. To savour the tender beauty of spring and the smell of life blossoming, to marvel at the colour of falling autumn leaves and abundant harvests grown in healthy soil. In this way, we would learn from the cycles of life, death and rebirth all around us. As Robin Wall Kimmerer notes, 'Even a wounded world is feeding us. Even a wounded world holds us, giving us moments of wonder and joy. I choose joy over despair. Not because I have my head in the sand, but because joy is what the earth gives me daily and I must return the gift.'*

The world is constantly remade, like the shifting particles of the Sahara. There is power in every small act, as when grains of sand eventually form a great dune. May our intentions be the wind, forming new constellations of life-affirming infrastructure. May abundant love be our compass. May our actions speak louder than words.

* * *

In these times of political upheaval, I find myself returning to one question: How can I become a good ancestor? This question guides me, through oscillating waves of connection, fear and surrender.

It's a question that requires me to sense and feel. To notice the world and allow it to touch me, rather than numbing, ignoring or tuning it out. Sometimes this is only possible for a few minutes at a time. Sensing and feeling takes practice in a world that conditions us to operate like consumerist zombies, living from the neck up – addicted to our productivity rather than tuning into ourselves, the land and each other. Daily embodiment or somatic practice is a soothing balm for this conditioning. Through cycles of blossoming, composting, grief and rest, I regularly reflect and experiment as well as receive feedback from trusted kin to pivot when needed. I try to hear the song that wants to be sung through me to support the web of life.

During a workshop with the artist Joy Mariama Smith, I learned the etymology of the word consent: it means sensing together. It struck me that it is very challenging to sense together if we cannot even sense ourselves. Perhaps that is why many cannot hear the cries of the Earth, or feel powerless when they do. Perhaps this is why the mainstream culture systemically dominates and controls the land, as well as our children. Perhaps this is why cycles of harm continue: we have lost the ability to feel that when we wound another, we are also wounding ourselves. The food we grow in depleted soil in turn depletes our gut microbiome. There is no separation. May we (re)learn cultures of consent and reciprocity to support the whole.

Until recently, I thought that courage could not exist in me if fear were present. A powerful chapter on courage in Prentis Hemphill's book *What It Takes To Heal* spoke to my tender heart, affirming that my courage can coexist with other emotions and can, with practice, become bigger than my fear.

* * *

Notice what sits alongside your fear. As you turn your attention inwards, become aware of any sensations in your body. If you detect any tension, or contraction, can you offer some gentle support or loving presence without trying to fix, bypass or make tension go away? Feel free to be with this for a few moments. Notice: Is there a part of you that longs to make a small offering towards change that can support your community or the wider world around you? To experiment with loving action within your sphere of influence. Examples could include protecting your local river from pollution, creating a composting system for your neighbourhood or organising against corporate harm.

Change is needed everywhere. Like adrienne maree brown outlines in her book, *Pleasure Activism*, I sense that moving from what sparks pleasure or interest in us can catalyse us to take steps to create the world we long for. I invite you to sense and feel your way into learning what small acts you can offer in service to the collective.

* Robin Wall Kimmerer, *Braiding Sweetgrass*, Minneapolis, MN 2013, p.327

Camille Barton is a writer, artist and embodied social justice facilitator. Rooted in Black Feminism, ecology and harm reduction, Camille is dedicated to creating networks of care and liveable futures.

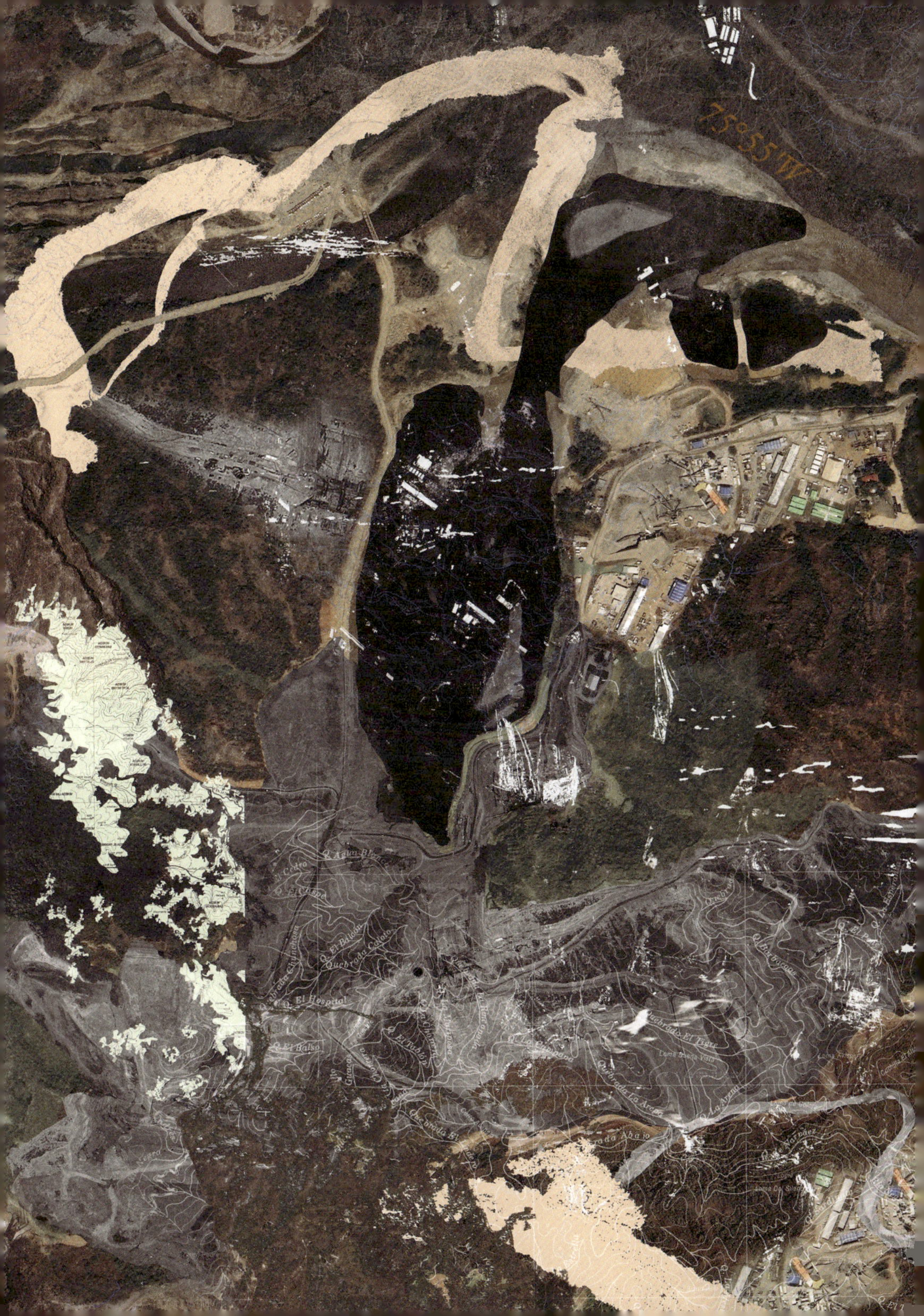
75°55'W
Q. Agua Blanca
El Cedro
Q. El Cuspe
Quebrada Chumbosa
Q. El Balcón
Quebrada Caloto
Q. El Hospital
Q. El Balso
Q. El Tablón

What happens to the land happens to us...

Radha D'Souza

The ecological crisis that we witness today has made us more willing to accept collective responsibility for the violence done to land – to everything below, on and above it. 'Humanity', we hear, is responsible for the Anthropocene, climate breakdown, and much else. *We*, 'the humanity', must treat the land with kindness and respect because – as a recent talk at Tate put it – 'what happens to the land happens to us'.*

Yet this way of framing the relationship of land and people is quintessentially Euro-American. For example, the International Rivers Network campaigned against large dams in the US because of the ecological consequences for land. The logic was similar: if land is harmed, we will be harmed. Groups campaigning against the Narmada Dam in India, in contrast, reversed the framing. Indigenous peoples – the peasant communities who had lived on the land since time immemorial – opposed the dam project because they lived on and protected the land. Outside the so-called West, in the 'Third World', which is really the two-thirds world, land and people continue to be inseparably entwined in rural areas. There, it is *harm to people* that ends up harming the land.

The most unique attribute of the human species is that we are concept-dependent, meaning we need conceptual resources to navigate the world around us. It is important that we periodically clean any conceptual cobwebs that may have gathered in our cognitive world. It is easy to forget that we humans are also part of Nature; when we say 'What happens to the land happens to us', it reinforces the dualism of Nature and people, objectifying Nature as something outside of ourselves. It 'others' Nature. It is time to invert the statement, and the thinking that underpins it.

The Nature-culture divide complicates the relationship of politics generally and the place of environment within it. For example, wars are waged in the name of promoting democracy (Iraq) and women's rights (Afghanistan), and to get rid of dictators (Libya, Syria). Modern warfare uses depleted uranium (Iraq, Afghanistan), nuclear weapons (Japan and Marshall Islands), and chemical weapons such as white phosphorus (Palestine), Agent Orange (Vietnam), and much else. Wars, focus on humans; remaining silent on ecology and environment. Can we assume that the deadly chemicals and weapons used in wars will harm only our human 'enemies', assuming they are our adversaries, and that they will do no harm to the land and Nature? When land is taken from Indigenous peoples for drilling or mining, or from peasant communities for building dams, they are first to fall defending the land. Before the land can be used in new ways, the guardians who have protected it for centuries must be removed forcibly, uprooted and evicted. If we save the Indigenous people, if we care about the peasants and herdsmen, the land will be safe. Casting an undifferentiated 'humanity' as adversaries conceals this reality. Equally, it conceals the identity of the real perpetrators of the Anthropocene and climate breakdown. It invites us to believe that miraculously the land can be saved without saving the human guardians of the land.

The truth is this: Nature does not care about us. If there is a nuclear war, for example, the planet will continue to revolve, the chemical reactions from the nuclear explosions will continue to happen. The land will still be there. We, 'humanity', will not.

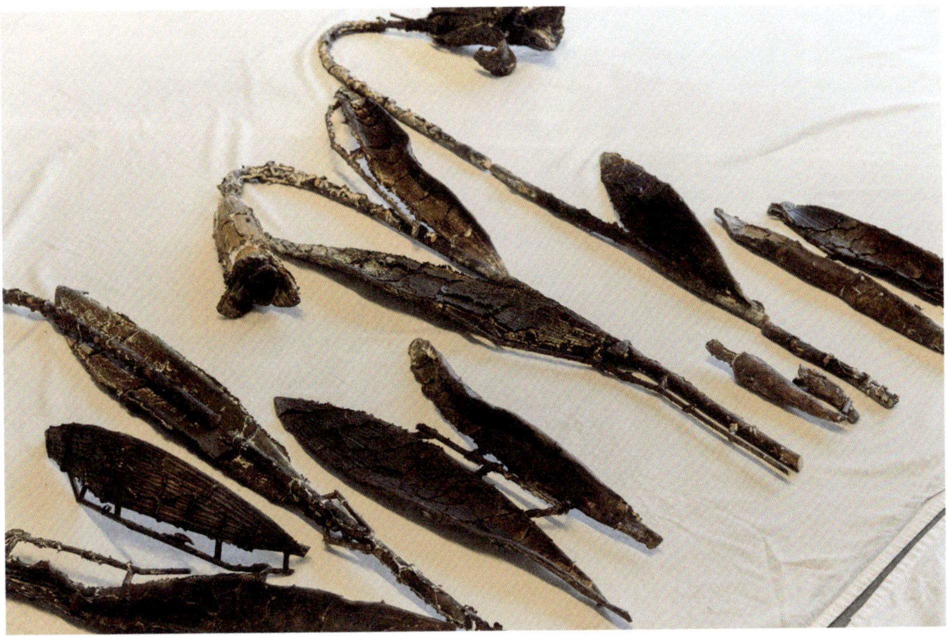

Abbas Akhavan, *Study for a Monument* 2022
Bronze and cotton sheets, dimensions variable. Tate. Purchased with funds provided by the Middle East North Africa Acquisitions Committee, the North American Acquisitions Committee, and Stephanie and Mark Robinson 2022. © Abbas Akhavan, photo © Tate Photography (Reece Straw). See also pp.34–5.

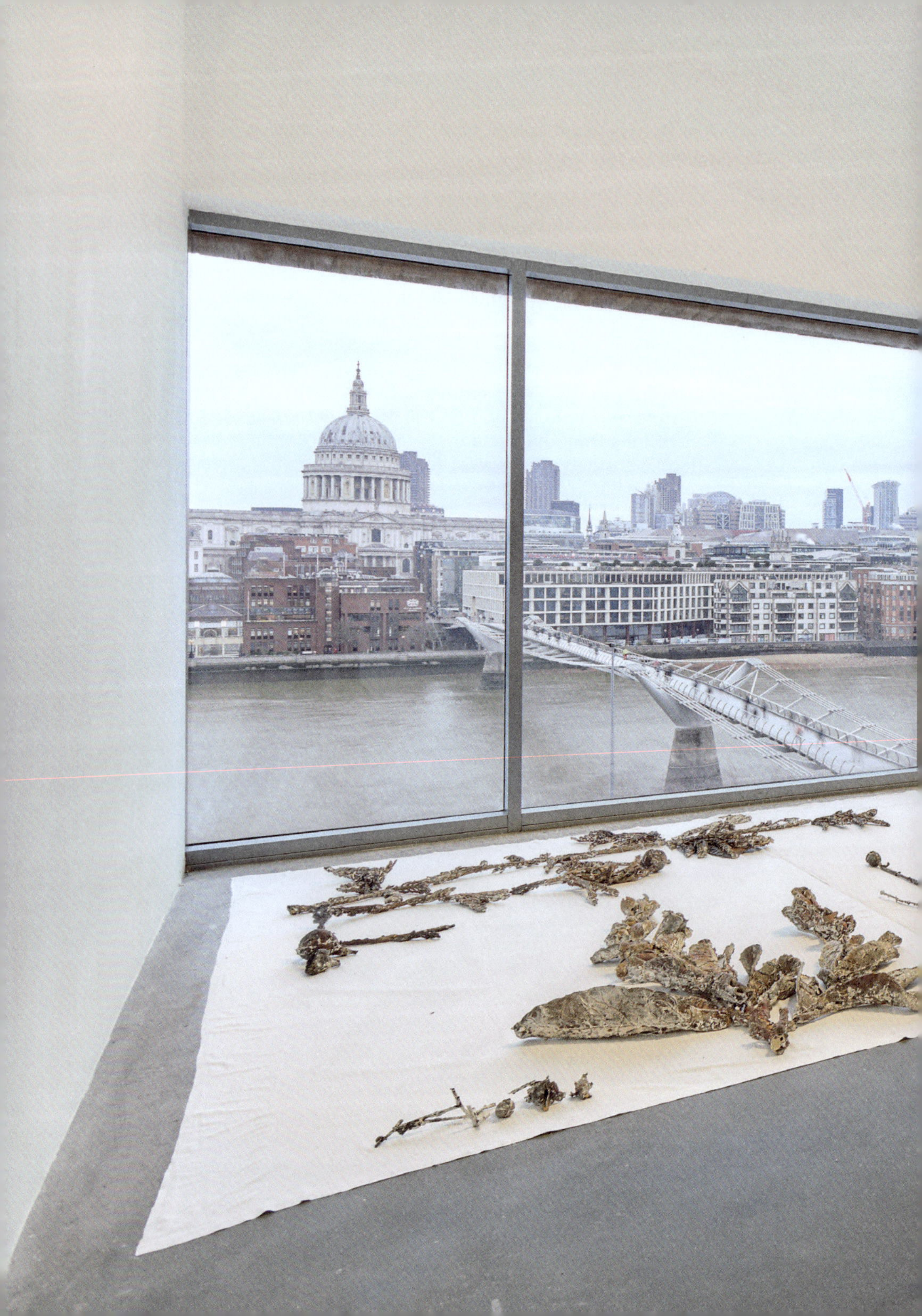

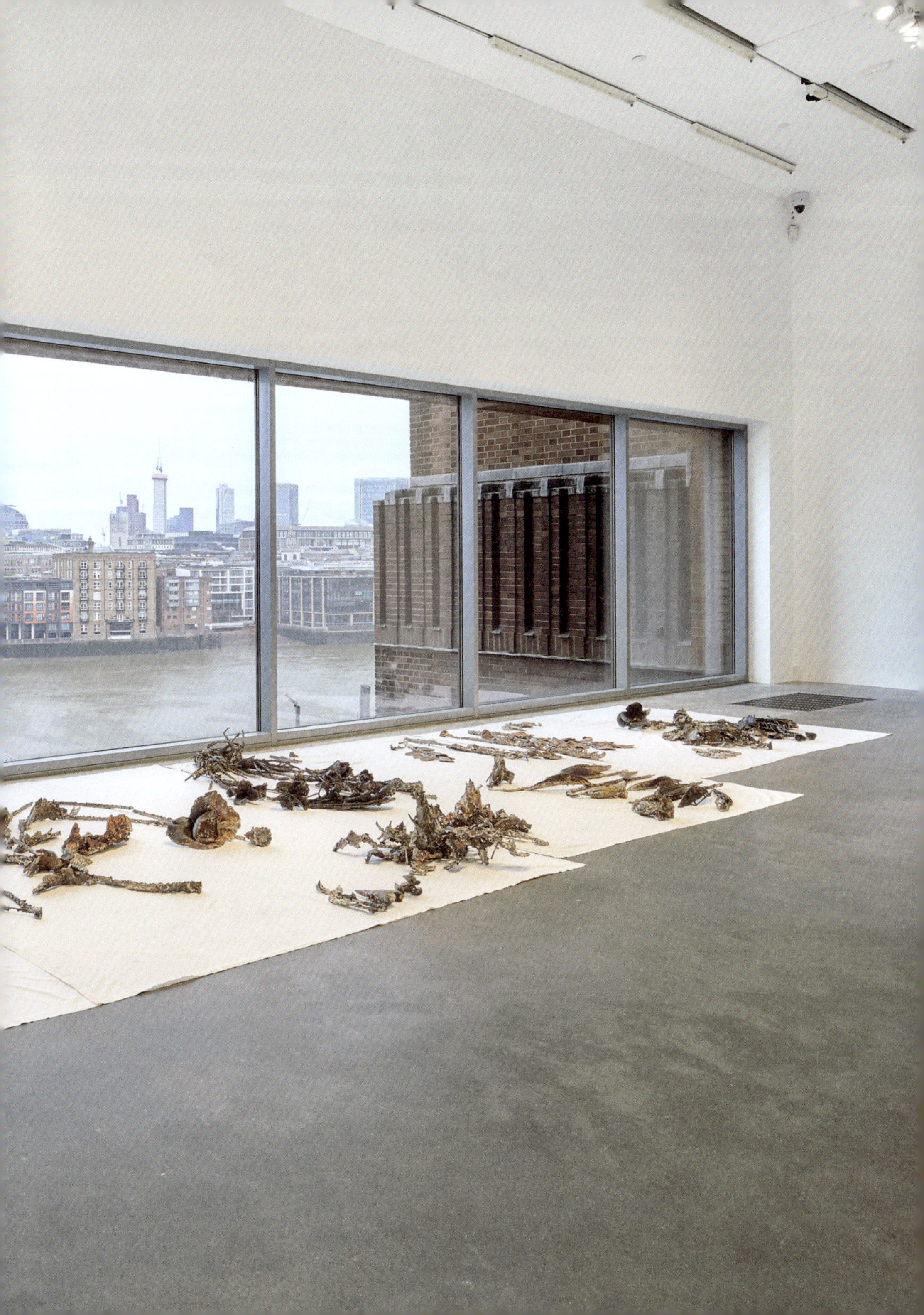

Human beings are unilaterally dependent on Nature for their existence, but Nature can exist without human beings. There are no human beings on Mars, or Jupiter. Planet Earth could become like one of those worlds. Therefore, it is for our sake and our collective existence that we need to make sure we do not nuke the world, and that we do not sacrifice the humans that look after and tend the land. It is important that we are not bluffed into believing that we can continue to throw people off their land and that abstract 'humanity' can care for it in their place. Which humans? Who lived and cared for the land before it was devastated, who was sacrificed before the land was harmed, and for whom? Which 'humans' devastated the land? We need to invert the way we see our relationship to land: to say, instead, What happens to us happens to the land...

* 'Hostile Environments: What Happens to the Land Happens to Us ...' was a one-day event held at Tate Modern on 20 February 2025, in partnership with the Visible Justice research hub at UAL: London College of Communication. It explored issues around environmental and social climate justice through performance, poetry and debates.

Radha D'Souza is Professor of International Law, Development and Conflict Studies at the University of Westminster and a social justice activist, barrister and writer from India.

Glossary

Ancestor
A person or being from whom one has descended. Many Indigenous peoples relate to their ancestors as entities who continue to bestow knowledge and protection for their descendants after their death. They are honoured through prayer, offerings and song, among other practices.

Capitalism
A globally dominant economic system characterised by private ownership of the means of production and operation. It is a system based on resource extraction, labour exploitation and profit accumulation. The term racial capitalism refers to the historical and ongoing exploitation of racialised people within economic systems. For example, enslavement and indentured labour show how racism acts as a central mechanism of capital accumulation.

Climate Emergency
The present situation where urgent action is required to reduce or halt climate breakdown and avoid the irreversible environmental damage resulting from it. Climate is the natural network of weather systems and patterns across the world. Human activity, largely the release of polluting gases from burning fossil fuel (coal, oil, gas), is impacting the climate, leading to extreme events such as high temperatures, drought, floods and wildfires.

Climate Justice
A movement and practice that frames the climate emergency as an ethical and political issue, rather than just environmental. Causes and effects of climate breakdown are approached through concepts of justice, particularly environmental and social. Climate justice examines concepts such as equality, human rights and the historical responsibility for climate breakdown, advocating for those who are most impacted.

Colonialism
The political and economic domination of a people or area by a foreign state or nation. It includes environmental practices and policies that harm people and their lands. Green colonialism often displaces Indigenous peoples from their lands under the guise of sustainability and conservation.

Custodian
Custodians, also known as stewards or guardians, take care of someone or something. Many Indigenous peoples and local communities act as custodians of their traditional lands and waters. They care for these entities and environments willingly, holding them in trust for future generations. Their custodianship relates directly to their cultural and spiritual practices.

Ecology
The relationships within living systems, between living organisms and their environments. An ecological perspective helps us better understand ecosystems and biodiversity, revealing the delicate web of connections that sustain us.

Ecocide
The reckless destruction or damage of ecosystems caused by human activities and which results in severe, long-term environmental harm. It includes actions like deforestation, pollution and industrial disasters. Calls to recognise ecocide as an international crime are increasing and aim to hold individuals, corporations and governments accountable.

Ecological anxiety
Ecological anxiety, also known as eco-anxiety or climate-anxiety, is defined by the Climate Psychology Alliance as heightened emotional, mental or somatic distress in response to dangerous changes in the climate system.

Ecological crisis
The ecological breakdown caused by human activities. It describes the ways in which the Earth's ecosystems are either severely damaged for several generations or entirely endangered. It goes beyond the climate crisis and involves the collapse of living systems and relations. The ecological crisis is inseparable from global capitalist and colonial structures, which treat nature as a resource for extraction and exploitation.

Ecological grief
Ecological grief, also known as eco-grief or climate grief, is the sense of loss that is felt in relation to experienced or anticipated environmental harm. This includes the loss of species, ecosystems, and landscapes due to climate breakdown and ecological destruction. A related term is climate trauma, which refers to the psychological distress experienced in response to these changes.

Eco-somatics
A growing field of research and practice that looks to understand our sense and awareness of our bodies in relation to our wider environment. It explores the interconnectedness between our embodied self and external environment and emphasises the link between the two.

Extractivism
The removal of natural resources particularly for export and profit. Extractivist practices are exploitative and environmentally and socially damaging for local communities. Extractivism is pervasive in the Global South and Arctic region and is linked to colonialism and the violation of Indigenous people's rights to their land.

Indigeneity
Indigeneity must be understood through Indigenous practices and thinking. It refers to being Indigenous to a land or territory and the relationships to history, culture and intergenerational knowledge this carries. This encompasses cultural and political subjectivities, worldviews, systems of governance, practices and relations to the land. Indigenous peoples face ongoing fights for self-determination, land rights, sovereignty and the recognition of injustices Indigenous communities lived through due to colonisation.

Land Defenders
Also known as environmental defenders or land protectors, Land Defenders stand up for the protection of ecologies and places that are threatened. Often these are the Land Defenders' homes or ancestral lands. Practices include demonstrations and advocacy against extractive and destructive state and corporate land developments.

Lifeworld
A concept that can describe our social, cultural and ecological lived experiences of the world. It challenges fixed, hierarchical distinctions between human and non-human, as well as nature and culture. Lifeworld encompasses relational, entangled and embodied understandings of the world.

Peasant communities/Peasants
This term has been reclaimed by agricultural workers who engage in subsistence farming and maintain close ties to the land and knowledges of the land. La Via Campesina, an international movement representing millions of small-scale farmers, understands peasant communities as crucial for resistance against exploitative capitalist systems and corporate agriculture. Peasant communities are essential to movements for food sovereignty.

Reciprocity
A framework in many Indigenous practices, embedded in the interconnectedness of all beings. In this context, reciprocity is ecological, relational and connected with the land. It emphasises respect and balance to enable collective well-being and the sustainability of life and relations. This is fundamentally different to individualistic understandings of reciprocity as transactional exchanges of goods and services for mutual benefit.

Sovereignty
A supreme power or authority, often over a territory. In contrast to this, many movements globally advocate for localised, land-based and grounded formations of sovereignty, or sovereignty from reliance on capitalist systems such as food sovereignty. This also includes Indigenous movements for sovereignty that emphasise the inherent and relational authority of Indigenous peoples to govern themselves, their lands and cultures.

Water Guardians
People or groups entrusted with the stewardship of a body of water, its care and protection. They often organise in direct opposition to the pollution, rechannelling or extraction of this body of water. Water guardianship is frequently grounded in understanding water as a living relative, which deserves respect and protection.